Adult Coloring Stress Relief

with
Calming Card Games

Spades

Copyright © Leaves of Gold Press 2015

All rights reserved. No part of this book may be reproduced or transmitted by any person or entity (including Google, Amazon or similar organisations) in any form or by any means, electronic or mechanical, including photocopying, recording or by any information storage and retrieval system, without prior permission in writing from the publisher.

Creator: Leaves of Gold Press - author.

Title: Adult coloring stress relief with calming card games: spades /
Leaves of Gold Press ;
Elizabeth Alger, illustrator.
Series: Adult coloring stress relief ; 2
ISBN: 9781925110869 (paperback)
Target Audience: Adult.

Image on reverse of cards: 'Pimpernel' by William Morris

BISAC categories:
Self-Help / Self-Management / Stress Management
Self-Help : Creativity
Body, Mind & Spirit / Mindfulness & Meditation

Scan the QR code to visit Leaves of Gold Press

ABN 67 099 575 078
PO Box 9113, Brighton, 3186, Victoria, Australia
www.leavesofgoldpress.com

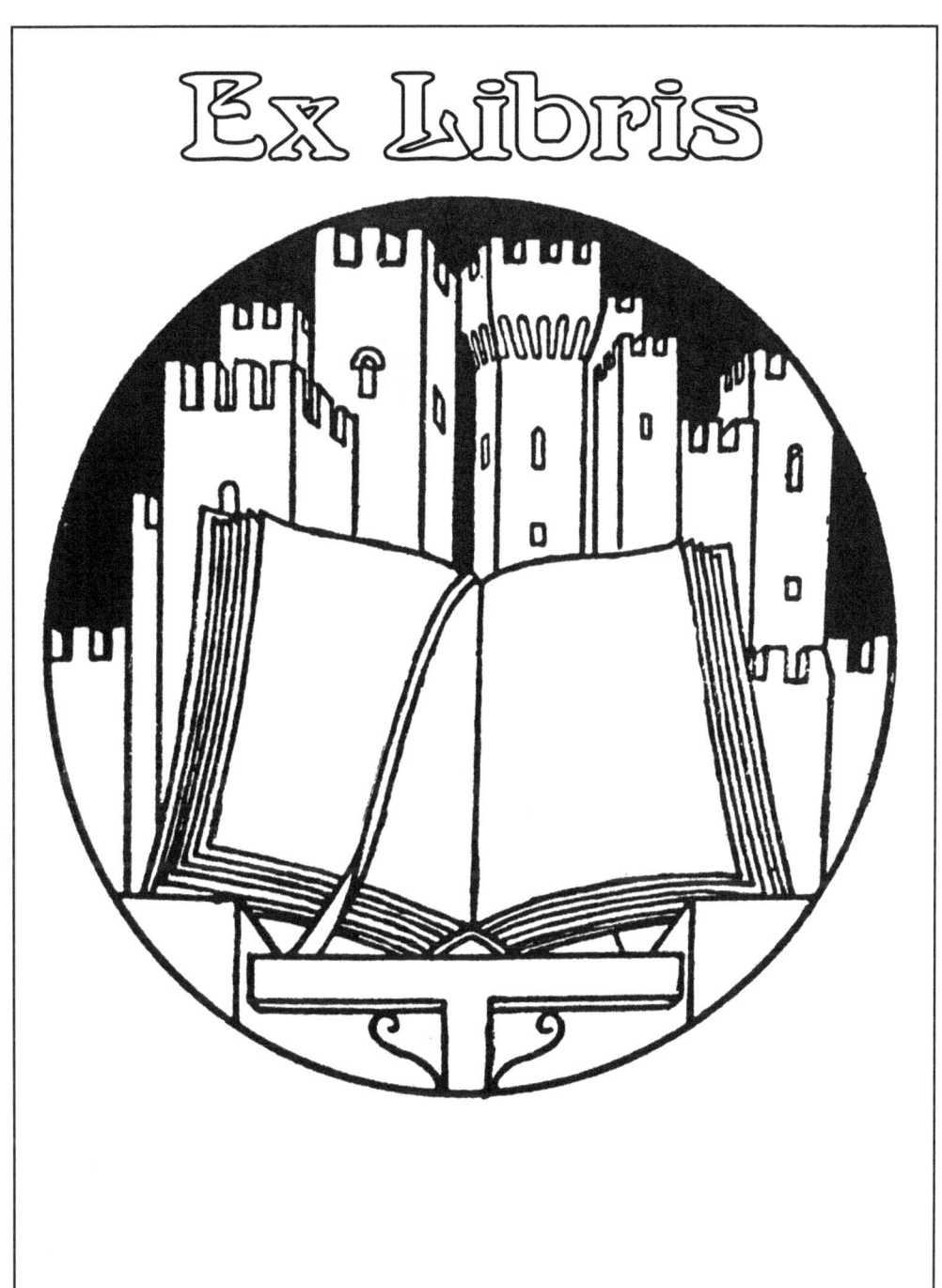

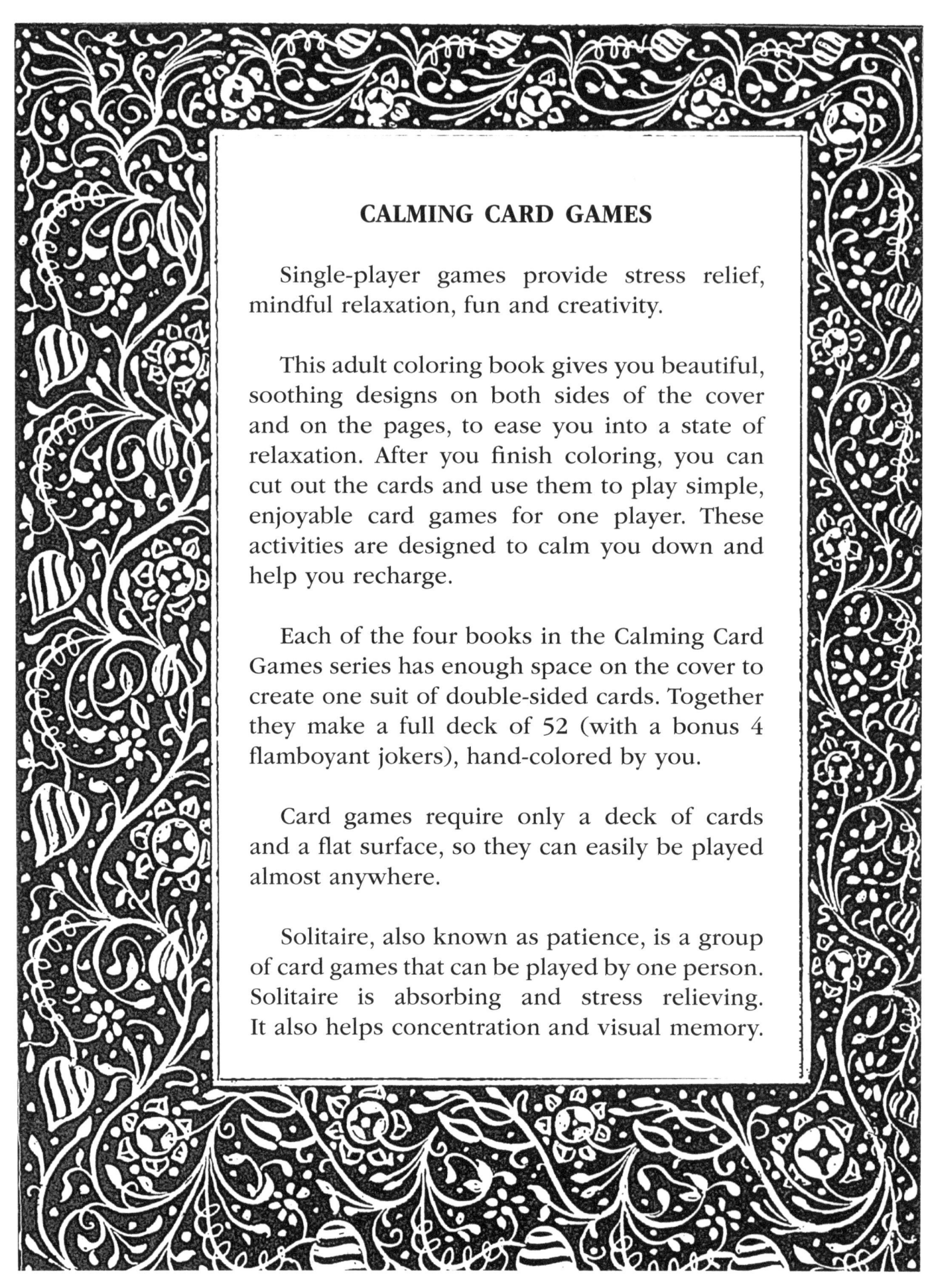

CALMING CARD GAMES

Single-player games provide stress relief, mindful relaxation, fun and creativity.

This adult coloring book gives you beautiful, soothing designs on both sides of the cover and on the pages, to ease you into a state of relaxation. After you finish coloring, you can cut out the cards and use them to play simple, enjoyable card games for one player. These activities are designed to calm you down and help you recharge.

Each of the four books in the Calming Card Games series has enough space on the cover to create one suit of double-sided cards. Together they make a full deck of 52 (with a bonus 4 flamboyant jokers), hand-colored by you.

Card games require only a deck of cards and a flat surface, so they can easily be played almost anywhere.

Solitaire, also known as patience, is a group of card games that can be played by one person. Solitaire is absorbing and stress relieving. It also helps concentration and visual memory.

Why use real cards?

Playing games with real cards instead of on a screen makes a huge difference to your health. When you use virtual cards on a light-emitting screen your eyes may become strained. Even more seriously — especially in the evenings — the blue-wavelength light from screens interferes with your body's melatonin production, thus disrupting your natural sleep rhythms. Looking at a screen before bed not only makes it harder to fall asleep, but also affects how drowsy or alert you are the following day.[1] Digital solitaire can also be highly addictive, unlike real solitaire.

Play soothing games with real cards to relieve stress and get a better night's sleep.

Join the natural stress relief trends sweeping the globe!

---

1 'Light-Emitting E-Readers Before Bedtime Can Adversely Impact Sleep.' Brigham and Women's Hospital. *Proceedings of the National Academy of Sciences, December 22, 2014.* Sleep deficiency has been linked to other health problems, including obesity, diabetes, and cardiovascular disease. Chronic melatonin suppression has also been associated with increased risk of certain cancers.

♠ THE SUIT OF SPADES ♠

In English-speaking countries the set of 52 French playing cards is the most popular. This comprises thirteen numerals of each of the four French suits; clubs, diamonds, hearts and spades. Each suit includes three 'court' or 'face' cards; king, queen and jack.

The Suit of Spades is derived from the Suit of Swords, one of the four suits of Latin-suited playing cards.

In tarot, the element of swords is air, and the Suit of Swords relates to the pure mind; thought and intellect.

In Italy and Spain the spades suit is still played as the Suit of Swords. The Italian word for sword is *spade* and the Spanish is *espadas*.

The Suit of Spades may represent the feudal class of aristocrats and nobles. It also corresponds to the Swiss-German Suit of Shields (*schilten*) and the German Suit of Leaves (*laub*).

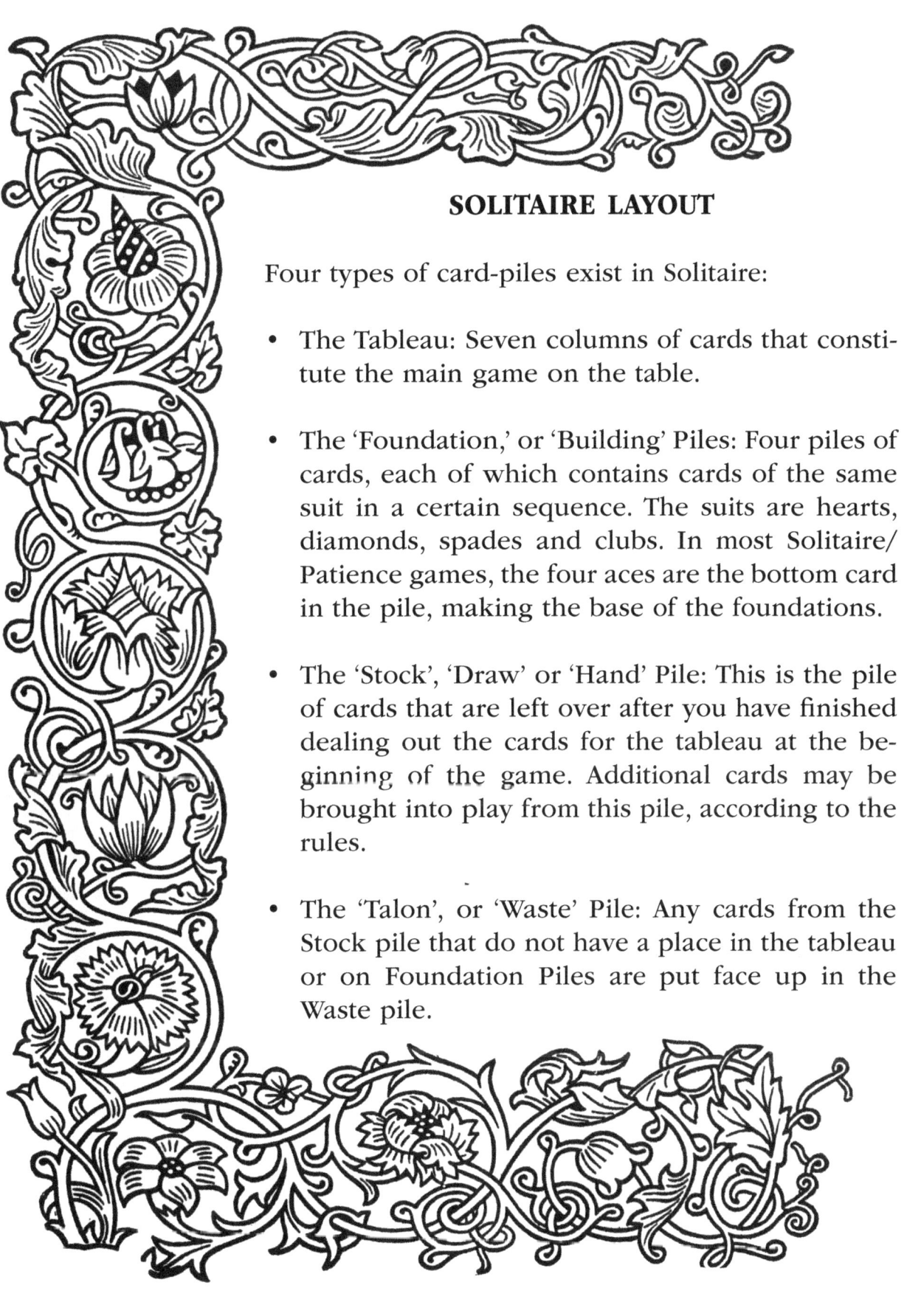

SOLITAIRE LAYOUT

Four types of card-piles exist in Solitaire:

- The Tableau: Seven columns of cards that constitute the main game on the table.

- The 'Foundation,' or 'Building' Piles: Four piles of cards, each of which contains cards of the same suit in a certain sequence. The suits are hearts, diamonds, spades and clubs. In most Solitaire/Patience games, the four aces are the bottom card in the pile, making the base of the foundations.

- The 'Stock', 'Draw' or 'Hand' Pile: This is the pile of cards that are left over after you have finished dealing out the cards for the tableau at the beginning of the game. Additional cards may be brought into play from this pile, according to the rules.

- The 'Talon', or 'Waste' Pile: Any cards from the Stock pile that do not have a place in the tableau or on Foundation Piles are put face up in the Waste pile.

Layout for Spiderette Solitaire

SOLITAIRE OR PATIENCE

Games of solitaire/patience generally involve re-arranging a layout of cards (called a 'tableau') with the aim of sorting them in some way.

There is a vast array of variations in one-player card games. The rules vary from simple to quite complex. Some use more than one deck of cards. This series of books, 'Adult Coloring Stress Relief with Calming Card Games' contains instructions for several of the most popular and relaxing games of solitaire, including:

- Klondike
- Accordion
- Flower Garden
- Spiderette
- Pyramid

Spiderette is similar to another type pf solitaire called Spider, except that it is played with a single deck of cards, instead of two. This makes the game a lot easier to win than Spider (therefore more relaxing!) and faster to play.
Instructions follow.

SPIDERETTE SOLITAIRE

Setup

Deal out the cards in the same tableau as for 'Klondike'.

The aim of the game is to arrange cards in a descending sequence from king to ace, within the tableau columns, regardless of suit.

In other words, you need to order the cards like this: king, queen, jack, 10, 9, 8, 7, 6, 5, 4, 3, 2, ace.

When you've created such a card sequence you move all the cards in that sequence to one of the four foundations. You have won the game when you have moved all 52 cards to the foundations as four distinct king-to-ace sequences.

Gameplay

You play Spiderette mainly by re-arranging the cards in the tableau columns. You are allowed to move any face-up card of any suit from the end of a tableau column to the end of another tableau column if it creates a descending sequence. For example you could move a 7 on top of an 8 or a 3 on a 4.

You are also allowed to move a 'fully packed' descending sequence of cards as a group to another tableau column, but only if they are cards of the same suit.

So for example if you have created a sequence of 5, 6, 7 and 8 of spades, you could move all four cards together to another column. For this reason it is wisest, as you are playing the game, to try to match cards of the same suit wherever possible. This makes it easier to win!

If you succeed in arranging a full descending sequence of cards from king to ace of the same suit, then you should remove it to one of the places you've reserved for 'foundations'.

You can fill empty tableau columns with any card or with a 'fully packed' descending sequence of cards of the same suit. When it becomes impossible to make any more useful moves on the tableau, deal out another card from the stock pile to each of the tableau columns. All the empty spaces in the tableau have to be filled before you are allowed to deal cards from the stock, even if you have to split up a sequence you have already arranged in order.

Four-suit Spiderette is the official version of the game, but it is not easy to win.

Variations of Spiderette

One-Suit Spiderette
   In this variation, sort out your deck of cards and play only with the spades. It makes the game very easy!
Two-Suit Spiderette
   Set aside the clubs and diamonds and play the game only with the spades and hearts.

Extra decks of cards are required to make up the numbers.

Spiderette Scoring

Simply winning or losing a game is fine, but it may not be as interesting as finding out how well you scored. In Spiderette you can win points according to the following rules.

To gain points:
Every time you flip over a face-down card, reward yourself with 150 points. However you are not allowed more than 3150 points at the most, for this move.

For moving a sequence of cards to the foundations in One-Suit Spiderette, give yourself 650 points. Do not exceed the maximum of 2600 points. In Two-Suit Spiderette you get 780 points for this move, not exceeding 3120 points. With the four-suit variation this move gives you 910 points, up to 3640 points.

ADULT COLORING STRESS RELIEF: THE SERIES

Book 1: Adult Coloring Stress Relief with Calming Paper Crafts

Book 2: Adult Coloring Stress Relief with Calming Card Games: Spades

Book 3: Adult Coloring Stress Relief with Calming Card Games: Hearts

Book 4: Adult Coloring Stress Relief with Calming Card Games: Diamonds

Book 5: Adult Coloring Stress Relief with Calming Card Games: Clubs

IS FOOD MAKING YOU SICK?

People all over the world suffer from histamine intolerance without being aware of it.

We itch, sneeze, suffer from joint pain, inflammation, sleep disorders, irritability, anxiety, bowel disease, diarrhea, flatulence, stomach pain, heartburn and acid reflux, nausea, bloating and other digestive problems, eczema, psoriasis, tissue swelling, urticaria (hives), itching skin, itching scalp, sinusitis, runny nose, puffy eyes, hay fever, asthma, and breathing difficulties, or endure tension headaches, migraines, fuzzy thinking, dizziness, irregular heartbeat, painful periods (women), sudden drops in blood pressure, faintness or flushing.

Symptoms may endure throughout our entire lives if we continue to consume large amounts of histamine without knowing it. Histamine is colorless, odorless and tasteless — undetectable except by scientific analysis, and yet crucial to our well-being. Individual histamine tolerance thresholds vary greatly.

The good news is, if we can understand what is happening and why, we can treat or prevent this widely unrecognized condition. By far the best way to treat histamine intolerance (HIT) is with diet. All foods with the potential to raise histamine levels should be avoided until your health improves significantly.

This book discusses HIT in depth, including causes, symptoms and therapies, backed by scientific research. Along with a list of foods to help HIT sufferers, it includes a wide range of recipes for everything from entrées to desserts.

Find out more at www.low-histamine.com

THE SLEEP-INDUCING BEDTIME STORY

Children sometimes find it hard to get to sleep.

What if you could read them a bedtime story incorporating powerful psychological methods to help them fall asleep quickly, easily and without drugs?

Psychological sleep induction techniques include:
• putting aside your thoughts until the following day
• breathing deeply
• slowing down
• imagining a descent with the sensation of sinking
• progressive muscle relaxation
• using sleep-triggering words
• visualizing a safe and peaceful place
• employing the 'infectiousness' of yawning.

Such methods are well-known and can be found in libraries or by searching for 'psychological sleep techniques' on the Internet.

This book also uses the hypnotic power of rhyme and rhythm. Songs and lullabies have traditionally been used to lull children to sleep. 'Hypnotic' poetry works in much the same way.

The poems in this book are in the relaxing, calming rhythm called 3/4 time, better known as 'waltz time'. All parents know that gentle, rocking rhythms can soothe a child.

The rhyming is as important as the rhythm.

Children love poems that rhyme. For them, rhyming words make poetry fun and memorable. Just as children respond to Forssen Ehrlin's sleep-inducing story of Roger the Rabbit (the inspiration for this book), so they can fall asleep while listening to the tale of Misti the Kitty.

 # 1 New Release on Amazon in 'Sleep Disorders'.

www.ingramcontent.com/pod-product-compliance
Lightning Source LLC
LaVergne TN
LVHW070951070426
835507LV00030B/3489